TURKEY

A *terra magica* BOOK

4.98

TURKEY

Edited by Hanns Reich

Text by Hans Leuenberger

Photographs by Klaus D. Franke, Ara Güler,
Helmut Bergtold and Others

HILL AND WANG

Published in the United States of America
by Hill and Wang, Inc.
International Standard Book Number: 0-8090-2200-1.
Library of Congress Catalog Card Number: 77-148233.
© 1970 Hanns Reich Verlag, Munich.
English translation copyright © 1971 by Joyce Clemow.
All rights reserved, including those of photographic
reproduction, reprint in whole or part,
and broadcast by radio and television.
Printed in Germany.

Far away in Turkey

These words were written by Johann Wolfgang von Goethe. Today, however, Turkey is no longer considered such a remote land. Munich is approximately only nine hundred miles by air from Istanbul, a city whose name has been changed in the course of history from Byzantium to Constantinople and then to its present name, Istanbul. A further nine hundred miles separates the Bosporus from the eastern frontier of this land, which is the size of Spain and Italy together. Four seas bathe the shores of the Turkish coast: the Aegean, the Mediterranean, the Sea of Marmara, and the Black Sea. Two high coastal mountain chains surround an immense highland plateau. The central area of this plateau is barren and desolate, similar to the basins of Central Asia. In the middle of this Anatolian tableland a volcanic cone known as Mount Erciyas (Erciyas Daği) rises to a height of almost 13,000 feet and is the highest mountain in the actual Mediterranean region. But it is overshadowed by Mount Ararat, towering to a height of 16,946 feet near the eastern Anatolian border. Mount Kavron (Kavron Daği), not far from the Turkish-Georgian (U.S.S.R.) frontier, just crests a height of 13,000 feet. In the region called the Armenian Highland there are at least one hundred and fifty peaks with altitudes greater than 13,000 feet. The geographical features of Turkey can be defined more clearly if Turkey is divided into its principal regions, which, moreover, are the same regions used when describing the country's tourist attractions.

The Black Sea Coast   The Black Sea Coast region extends inland for 60 to 120 miles, ascending from the coast into the Pontic Mountains, a high coastal mountain chain which provides this region of Anatolia with an abundant year-round rainfall. The moist climate is conducive to the cultivation of tea plants. The area is densely populated up to an altitude of approximately 1,650 feet. It is a fertile parkland renowned for its forests of rhododendrons and groves of hazelnut bushes, the latter making Turkey the main supplier of hazelnuts in the world, after Spain and Sicily. The main port of export is Trabzon (the ancient Greek city of Trapezus). Zonguldak and Karabük are flourishing industrial centers with coal mines, iron foundries, and steelworks.

The Marmara Region   The Marmara region is hilly and overgrown with low thorn shrubs which extend over the interior portion of the region into the steppe of the central plateau. The densely populated area is mainly industrial. Beyond Bursa, in former times capital of the Ottoman Empire, Mount Olympus (Ulu Dağ) stands about 8,000 feet above sea level. People nowadays use it as a winter ski resort. Istanbul is situated on the northern coast of the Sea of Marmara. With hundreds of mosques and the oldest Christian church and largest Muslim house of worship as symbols of its magnificent history, Istanbul lies at the crossroads of two continents.

The Aegean Region   The Aegean region is completely oriented toward the sea, and the moist sea breezes penetrate deep into the inland districts. There, in the fertile soil, figs, raisins, and tobacco thrive. These local products, which have attained a world-wide reputation, are exported through the port of Izmir. The city of Izmir (Smyrna) will soon have a population of a half million people.

The Mediterranean Area   The Mediterranean area extends inland for 120 miles. The surrounding mountain ranges stretch down to the coast and block the moist sea breezes from blowing into the inland districts. This partly subtropical agricultural region with flourishing banana trees has seen the development of some prosperous centers, such as Adana (on the banks of the Seyhan River), Ceyhan, Mersin (İçel), and Iskenderun (Alexandretta).

Central Anatolia   Central Anatolia is completely surrounded by high mountain chains which shelter it from the coastal winds. It is a highland plateau situated at an altitude of 3,000 feet. It has a characteristic continental climate with a rainfall of about only twelve inches per year in parts. There are some extensive pasturelands, for goats and sheep in particular. In the past this area was covered by vast forests. From March until June the highland steppe is transformed into a garden of flowers stretching as far as the eye can see. In addition to wild tulips (they are a native plant of Anatolia) there are unending carpets of poppies, gladioli, and many other plants familiar to us in our own gardens. Close by, wild almond and pear trees blossom with flowers of pale pink and brilliant white. By July all that remains is some grayish-green thistle along the road-sides. Just as in the southern Ukraine, thornbushes get ripped out of the ground by dust storms and roll along like enormous matted balls over this steppe, which has now become a wasteland.

6

In the middle of this arid steppe lies Ankara, the new capital of Turkey. In just fifty years it has become a city of a million inhabitants. Konya, the former capital of the Seljuk kingdom, still stands; while Eskişehir, situated in the lignite mining district to the west of Ankara, has developed into an industrial city. East of Ankara, in the heartland of the steppe, are Kayseri and Sivas, the former renowned for its mausoleums and its great caravansaries of ancient times and the latter famous for its rug-weaving industry.

Eastern Anatolia   Generally speaking, Eastern Anatolia comprises the mountainous region east of the Euphrates, formerly called the Armenian Highland. This sparsely wooded region with Erzurum as its economic center, has hardly been touched by technology. Lake Van is also situated in Eastern Anatolia.

Southeastern Anatolia   The corn-growing country of Southeastern Anatolia, characterized by long hot summers, lies in the plains leading to Syria. The cities of Mardin, Raman, Diyarbekir, and Urfa are located in this region. The frontier with Syria is demarcated by the Baghdad Railway, which, with the exception of a branch to Aleppo, passes through Turkish national territory.

Historical Regions   In addition to the geographical areas listed above, Turkey can be subdivided into various historical regions:

Bithynia	in the central and lower Sakarya basin.
Cappadocia	west of the Euphrates, in the Ceyhan, Seyhan, and Kizil Irmak basins.
Caria	the highland plains behind the southern coast of the Aegean Sea.
Cilicia	on the southern slopes of the central Taurus Mountains.
Commagene	east of the Taurus Mountains, between Cappadocia and the Euphrates.
Lycaonia	in Central Anatolia, north of the central Taurus Mountains.
Lycia	on the southern coast, west of the Taurus Mountains
Lydia	the mid west-coast and the area bordering the Gediz River.
Mysia	in Western Anatolia, along the northern Aegean coast.

7

Paphlagonia	situated around the lower and middle course of the Kizil Irmak, in the central part of the Black Sea Coast.
Phrygia	between Mysia, Bithynia, and Pisidia (in the center of Western Anatolia).
Pisidia	situated among the well-drained inland basins and valleys which empty into the southern Aegean Sea (north of the western Taurus Mountains).

When Turkish people travel today, they pass through districts whose names attest to epochs in Anatolian history. This is a constant reminder to them that their role in the history of Asia Minor began very late — scarcely a thousand years ago, which is a short period in the life of a nation.

Climate In Asia Minor, situated between the Sahara and Siberia, the Caucasus and the Mediterranean, and between Mount Ararat and the Turkish "Rivera," there are numerous variations in climate. As a general rule, however, Turkey is divided into three climatic zones:

THE BLACK SEA: The summers are not extremely hot, but the winters are long and cold. This region has an abundant year-round rainfall and an average annual temperature of 57°F. It has a mean winter temperature of 43°F, rising to 74°F in the summer months.

THE HIGHLAND PLATEAU: This region is characterized by a continental climate. Warmth which is accumulated in the ground during the day is able to radiate out thanks to the dry, clear air of this type of climate. During the coldest month of the year the temperature always falls below 32°F. Sivas, situated at 3,500 feet above sea level, has a mean temperature of 23°F in January; and Ankara, at an altitude of 1,125 feet, has an average temperature of 29°F during the same month. In summer the mean temperature for the month of July climbs to 64°F in Sivas and to 74°F in Ankara. The average annual temperature is between 46°F and 52°F.

THE MEDITERRANEAN COAST: This zone has a characteristic Mediterranean coastal climate. The average temperature of the coldest month always stays a few degrees above freezing point (32°F). In Istanbul the mean temperature for the month of January is 39°F. Izmir and Antalya have mean temperatures of 46°F and 50°F, respectively, during the month of January. The average temperature during the summer months is approximately 77°F. In July Istanbul has a mean temperature of 74°F, Izmir 81°F, and Antalya 82°F.

The royal family depicted in a Roman relief sculpture on Theodosius' pedestal in Istanbul.

Antalya has an annual rainfall of 40 inches, of which, 31 inches fall during a four-month period from December through March, and only half an inch falls during the summer months (June, July, and August). In Istanbul more than half of the annual rainfall (29 inches per year) falls in the winter months, from December to March. Ankara, with its continental climate, has a rainfall of only 14 inches per year, and the heaviest downpours occur in early summer. In May alone, 2 inches of rain may fall. The Black Sea Coast has its heaviest rainfall in the autumn. Half of Trabzon's annual rainfall occurs between September and December.

History   In Turkey today there are two banks whose very names are evidence of the determination of the Turks to emphasize the ancient history of Anatolia in spite of the other great civilizations which have since intervened. The Sümer Bank and the Eti Bank have been named after the ancient Sumerians and Hittites.

9

A major part of Turkish history took place between the Altai, China, and Iran. It was only at the beginning of modern times, in the year 1453, that the Turks, led by Mohammed II, captured Constantinople and renamed it Istanbul. For four hundred years Byzantium (Constantinople) had been able to hold out against the Seljuk Turks, who had come from Iran and settled in Eastern Anatolia. But the Byzantines, heirs of the Roman Empire, were not powerful enough to maintain the vast territory left them by the Romans.

The Turks have occupied a difficult position in Europe, and the distorted picture of modern Turkish history still persists in many places. The peoples subjugated by the Turks have all re-emerged since the fall of the Turkish Empire and have been able to develop into individual nations. The same cannot be said of the Moors in Spain, who were driven out of Iberia. Saint Sophia (Aya Sofia), the oldest Christian church, was not destroyed by the Muslim Turks. They merely added minarets and converted the church into a mosque. Without their great quality of tolerance, the Turks would have been unable to govern their immense kingdom, especially when their rulers also assumed leadership of the Muslim faith and made Istanbul the center for Pan-Islamism.

The long war being waged between Europe and Islam became a holy war against the Turks after they had defeated the Arabs. The aim of the Crusades, however, was not to destroy the Turkish Empire but rather to gain access to Christ's Sepulcher in the Holy Land. Obviously, though, the European powers did combine political motives with their religious ventures.

Although it is an awesome task, the history of Anatolia should be analyzed from several different viewpoints. The following survey will try to present a comprehensive picture of this history. Turkey is one of the most important archaeological sites on earth. However, the Turks, the most recent conquerors of this land, do not have as strong an interest in this aspect of their country as the Europeans. For example, many European tourists will purchase a replica of the Trojan horse carved out of wood or a painting of the beautiful Helen of Troy. But the Turks at the present time are preoccupied with "uniting their new national character with the land they live on," as Jean Paul Roux has written. This "consolidation" is taking place along the coasts, on the mountains and steppes, in the forests, and among all the diverse peoples who today call themselves Turks. Kemal Atatürk, "the Father of

Portion of the largest Urartaean inscription, carved into a cliff at Van. It bears Assyrian cuneiform characters and dates from the reign of King Argishti I.

Turkey," once honored a Turkish wrestler by giving him a villa because his victories had helped re-establish the image of the "strong Turk" (strong as a Turk). Nations like the Hungarians, Bulgarians, or even the Americans and the Australian immigrants have settled in countries with no great prior civilizations. But the Turks in Asia Minor live in a land impregnated with a great cultural history. Yet at the same time they have appeared to the rest of the world as barbarians and uncivilized nomads whose cultural achievements in Central Asia and Iran have gone completely unnoticed. So the Turks are trying to solve the problems and correct the misconceptions which now confront them.

The nomadic Turks did not invade Asia Minor solely as warriors. They also settled there with their families, who mixed with the native peoples on the peninsula and slowly intermarried with them. It is difficult to estimate how long this process took.

In the Ottoman Empire (until the twentieth century) scarcely any sub- 11 jects of the Sultan called themselves Turks. They simply identified themselves as Muslim or even "Ottoman" – a fitting term for a community united by faith and unconcerned about "race." But after the collapse of the Ottoman Empire and the wars of intervention, and after the Armenian attempt to become independent had been ruthlessly suppressed, one group of people still remained on the Asia Minor peninsula. Mindful of the ancient civilizations of the Sumerians and the Hittites, which were founded on this very land, they chose to establish their own nation and to call themselves Turks. The father of this Turkish nation was Atatürk.

Chronology

6500 B.C.	Neolithic age settlements. The frescoes south of Konya (Çatalhöyük) are among the most ancient in the world.
3500 B.C.	Founding of Troy I.
1800–1500 B.C.	The Hittites founded a kingdom between the eastern Black Sea and the Syrian plains. The capital was Hattuşaş (officially designated as Boğazköy today), near Ankara. Their western neighbors were the Hurrians, an Anatolian race who had built an empire between the Euphrates and the Mediterranean. Through the Hurrians, whose culture had been strongly influenced by Babylon, the Hittites also came into contact with the Babylonian civilization. Egyptian chroniclers have described a one-sided picture of the Hittites, but this picture was recently corrected when excavations unearthed some remarkable artistic works belonging to this mysterious race. The Hittites spoke a dialect characterized by suffixes (like Turkish). This language has now been deciphered. In the Hittite Museum at Ankara some wonderful art treasures of the Hittite civilization are on display. There are lions carved out of stone, bronze sundials, and many other objects which will lend the support of a millenium-old history to a developing Turkish nation.
1298–1283 B.C.	Battles between Pharaoh Ramses II and the Hittites, who had extended their sovereign territory deep into the Syrian plains.
1250 B.C.	Partial successors of the Hittites were the Phrygians, who had built an empire in Anatolia which ultimately extended from the territory controlled by Babylon to the Euphrates. The center of this Phrygian state was situated in the upper Sakarya basin, where Gordium, the capital, was located. The Phrygians came into contact with the Greeks and adopted their writing. The Indo-European Phrygians had emigrated from the Caucasian region and in the course of time adopted some of the Greek deities. Their most famous king was Midas.
1000 B.C.	Greek immigration to Asia Minor increased. In the north the Aeolians invaded from Thessaly and Boeotia and founded colonies along the southern coast as far as Smyrna. The Ionians captured a part of their territory from them. An "Ionian Union" was formed, with a religious center at Cape Mycale (Poseidon Helikonios).

The Dorian immigrants settled primarily at Halicarnassus.

The Greek immigrants tried unsuccessfully to penetrate further inland. But they were forced by the local inhabitants to organize themselves into city states and entrench themselves behind city walls. This is how the *polis* originated and it later became the model for Greece.

6th Century B.C.   To the east the Lydians were forming a kingdom and they proceeded to overthrow the Phrygians. Sardis, built on the Hermus River, was their capital. The downfall of the Assyrian Empire encouraged the Lydians to expand their kingdom eastward until they encountered the Medes.

546 B.C.   The Persian king Cyrus II invaded Anatolia and defeated the Lydians (led by their king Croesus).

The Carians established their own kingdom on the southern coast.

Cyrus the Great, the victorious Persian king, became the ruler of Asia Minor and divided the sovereign territory into four satrapies (provinces): Cilicia, Cappadocia, Lycia, and Ionia.

513 B.C.   Darius seized the straits and took control of trade with the territories around the Black Sea. Until that time trading had been controlled by the Greeks living in the coastal cities of Asia Minor.

499–494 B.C.   Revolt of the Greek coastal cities. The Ionians tried to conquer Sardis with the help of two dozen ships dispatched from Athens and additional auxiliary forces. They were defeated by the Persians and again subjugated.

490 B.C.   The Persians tried to take revenge on Athens, landed an expeditionary corps in Greece, and met with defeat near Marathon.

468 B.C.   Following a period of internecine fighting the Greeks living in the coastal cities of Anatolia and their allies in the mother country succeeded in breaking the power of the Persians. But disunity among the Greeks and Athens' attempt to assume leadership of the Union gave the Persians the opportunity to take control of the Greek cities of Asia Minor once again.

334 B.C.   One year was sufficient for Alexander the Great to seize all of Asia Minor from the Persians. Phrygia became the first Macedonian province in Anatolia.

333 B.C.   After crossing the Taurus Mountains, Alexander the Great encountered the Persians, led by King Darius III, at Issus, not far from Iskenderun, and secured his power in Asia Minor with a decisive victory.

323 B.C.   Alexander the Great died of malaria in Baghdad, where he was preparing an expedition against the Arabs. His premature death stopped the

Hellenic civilization from encompassing the Arabic race also. The destiny of Anatolia naturally changed considerably after the death of this great commander-in-chief.

311 B.C. Quarrels broke out among the generals over the division of the empire. Finally the successors of the Egyptian Ptolemy intervened. Anatolia was subsequently incorporated into the Seleucid kingdom. However, some independent kingdoms, such as the Greek kingdom of Pergamum, were formed in Anatolia. The kingdom of Bithynia was "small but rich." Its king seems to have summoned the Galatians into the country for military support in his struggle against the Seleucids. This Celtic race of Galatians proves that "hordes" moved in not only from Asia but also from Europe and took part in some fierce invasions. There were several cities flourishing in Western Anatolia, one of which was Byzantium, now called Istanbul.

133 B.C. Attalus III of Pergamum, whose forefathers had concluded an alliance with Rome, had no heir to his throne and so bequeathed his kingdom to the Roman Senate. Rome extended its possessions in Asia Minor and tried to annex Phrygia in spite of resistance from Mithridates VI, ruler of the Pontic kingdom on the Black Sea.

103–89 B.C. Mithridates managed to defeat the Romans, seized all of Asia Minor, and landed in Greece.

86 B.C. Sulla, the Roman general, defeated the Persian king, and Rome again occupied a part of Anatolia.

64 B.C. Pompey defeated Mithridates in the Lycus valley. One year later the king of Pontus was murdered. Pompey then divided Anatolia into the two provinces of Pontus and Cilicia. The various peoples became more unified.

42 B.C. Mark Anthony assumed leadership of the Eastern Roman Empire.

31 B.C. Octavius defeated Mark Anthony at Actium and incorporated this Eastern Empire back into the Roman Empire.

The first two hundred years after the birth of Christ brought prosperity to Anatolia. The inhabitants were pronounced Roman citizens by the emperor Caracalla.

A.D. 285 Rule of Roman Empire divided by Diocletian between himself, keeping the eastern half, and Maximian, who took the western half.

324–337 Assumption of complete power by Constantine the Great.

330 Founding of Constantinople in the place of Byzantium.

395 Division of the Roman Empire was complete.

476	Rome fell into the hands of the barbarians. Constantinople became the sole capital of the Eastern Roman Empire (with a series of emperors who reigned until 1453), while the Western Roman Empire had already been destroyed by 476.
637	The Arabs appeared on the scene. In 627 Heraclius had defeated the Persians, and his empire extended as far as Egypt and Mesopotamia. The hellenization of Anatolia began. The Greek language supplanted Latin. The Roman title of *emperor* was replaced by the Greek title *basileus* (king). Shortly before the death of Heraclius, the Arabs advanced westward and captured Syria, Palestine, Mesopotamia, and Armenia.
674	Siege of Constantinople by the Arabic fleet. The naval battle between the Byzantians and the Arabs recurred every year for five years.
1050	The Turkish Seljuks occupied Iran. Ten years later they appeared in Anatolia.
1071	The Seljuks captured the Byzantine emperor Diogenes. Founding of the first Seljuk emirate at Iznik (Nicaea).
1097–1204	Crusades. Antioch captured by the Crusaders.
1204	Capture of Constantinople by the Crusaders.
1242–1258	The Mongols invaded Anatolia, overthrew the Seljuk rulers, and took control of the Seljuk kingdom.
1270–1300	The Byzantians recaptured Constantinople. Various Turkish empires were formed in Central Anatolia.
1300	Osman I, founder of the Osmanli dynasty, seized more cities from the Byzantians.
1326	Orkhan, oldest son of Osman, captured Bursa, which he chose as the capital of his newly founded small kingdom.
1366	Murad I, son of Orkhan, captured Adrianople and set it up as his capital. And so the Turks had established a foothold in Europe.
1396	The Ottomans advanced to Sofia and captured the city. Constantinople was thus confined within its own walls.
1400–1402	Second Mongolian invasion. Tamerlane defeated the Ottoman army and placed the former local Turkish rulers back on their thrones. A tribute was levied on Constantinople.
1453	Capture of Constantinople by Mohammed II, who renamed the city Istanbul and established it as the capital of the Ottoman (Osman) Empire.
1461	The Ottomans extended their empire along the Black Sea coast and northward to Serbia.

1512–1520	Sultan Selim I defeated the Persians and seized Armenia and South-eastern Anatolia (Diyarbekir). His victories over the Mamelukes led to the annexation of Syria, Palestine, and finally Egypt.
1529	Suleiman the Magnificent (1520–1566), under whom the Ottoman Empire saw its greatest territorial expansion, laid siege to Vienna after occupying Hungary. Vienna withstood the attack and the Viennese found a large number of sacks of coffee among the booty – and so the first Viennese coffeehouses were opened.
1533	Suleiman captured Mesopotamia and Azerbaijan.
1535	The Turkish corsairs occupied Algeria and Tunis. Malta repulsed the Ottoman attack.
1566	Another siege of Vienna. Suleiman died of a heart attack in Szigetvár, whereupon the Turks again retreated from Vienna.
1570	The capture of Cyprus by the Ottomans (led by Selim II) united an aroused Christendom against Islam. In the "disaster at Lepanto" the Turkish fleet was defeated by the Spanish and Venetians. The Turkish language, which the Seljuks had brought with them as their national dialect, gradually supplanted Persian.
1683	Another unsuccessful attempt to take Vienna.
1682–1725	Peter the Great of Russia seized the Crimean peninsula from the Ottomans, and attempted to take possession of the straits and thus have access to the Mediterranean, an old dream of the Russians. The power of the sultans was gradually being weakened by powerful eunuchs and the grand vizier.
1774	Russia obtained free passage through the Dardanelles. The weakened Ottoman Empire entered into an alliance with France and England to protect itself against Russia. Napoleon's campaign against Russia brought a temporary reprieve for the Ottomans. But when he made plans to conquer Egypt and Palestine as well, the Ottomans realized that he was a threat to them too.
1802	Peace treaty between France and the Ottoman Empire.
1808–1839	Mahmud II tried to disband his Christian mercenary soldiers (janis-saries). When they attempted to prevent this, he ordered his artillery to fire their dreaded Turkish cannons on them.
1853	Another Russo-Turkish war over the Crimea. England and France fought on the side of the Turks.
1856	Russian defeat decreed in the Treaty of Paris.
1878	The peace treaty of San Stefano was signed. After another Russo-

Turkish conflict this treaty decreed that the Ottoman Empire was to lose almost all of its European possessions.

1908 Formation of the Young Turks movement, which forced the sultan to fight on the side of Germany in World War I. The ultimate aim of the Young Turks movement was to found a Grand Turkish Empire which would include all the Turkish people (Turkmen, Uzbeks, Kazaks, formerly called Uighurs), the Turkish-speaking Sarts, the people of East Turkestan (formerly called Kirghizes). This dream came to an abrupt end when Germany was defeated by the Allies at the end of World War I. During World War II Hitler also promised the Turks a Grand Turkish Kingdom in return for their support. After he had persuaded the Crimean Tartars to fight with him against Stalin, he refused to keep his promise of a Tartar Crimean state and thereby showed the Turks that the Grand Turkish Kingdom they were being promised would, in fact, be an "imperial state" controlled by Hitler. The Turks remained neutral and the seizure of Caucasia by the German Empire failed to occur. The result: Stalingrad. The defeat of the German army at Stalingrad served to show the strategic importance of Asia Minor in international politics. The distribution of land among the peasants has allowed them to become owners of Turkish soil, which they are now always ready to defend. Internal unrest stemming from the newly developed industrial regions or from intellectual circles or emanating from the large cities disturbs the rural districts before anywhere else. Strategically, the position of Asia Minor has changed in that it now has a highway system built with American aid. All-weather roads have been constructed, so now Turkey must be supplied with motorized defense weapons. Any enemy is now able to drive over these roads, which were once dirt tracks and during the rainy season were virtually impassable, thus protecting an inaccessible, uncultivated land.

1919 Kemal Atatürk (born 1881) (previously known as Mustafa Kemal Pasha) was appointed commander-in-chief in the war against the Allies, who had occupied the country (English, French, Greeks, etc.).

1920 The Great National Assembly which convened at Ankara named Mustafa Kemal president of the Turkish Republic. In the Treaty of Sèvres, Sultan Mohammed VI had agreed to the division of Anatolia among the Allies. Kemal Pasha set about recapturing Asia Minor militarily.

1923 Treaty of Lausanne. The Allies left Istanbul. The Republic of Turkey 18 was proclaimed, with Ankara as the capital, and Kemal Pasha (Atatürk, "Father of Modern Turkey") was elected president. Major reforms: Introduction of the Roman alphabet with some additional symbols. Women were granted equal rights. Abolition of polygamy. The Gregorian calendar was introduced. Sunday, instead of the Muslim Friday, became the day of rest. Abolition of the veil and the fez. Adoption of the Swiss civil code, the German penal code, and the European commercial code.

1938 Death of Atatürk. His successor: Ismet Inönü, his best friend.

1952 Turkey became a member of the North Atlantic Treaty Organization.

1961 Adoption of a new constitution.

This last decade has been characterized by construction, financed with Western aid, and the strategic improvement of the country. Relations with Greece were discontinued because of the disagreement over the destiny of Cyprus, where a Turkish minority and a Greek majority confront each other.

The rapid development of tourism assures the country of a major source of supplementary revenue and helps refute many of the prejudices which we in the Western world hold about *"ces sacrés Turcs"* ("these confounded Turks!").

Photo captions in foldout section at the end of the book.

2

14

16

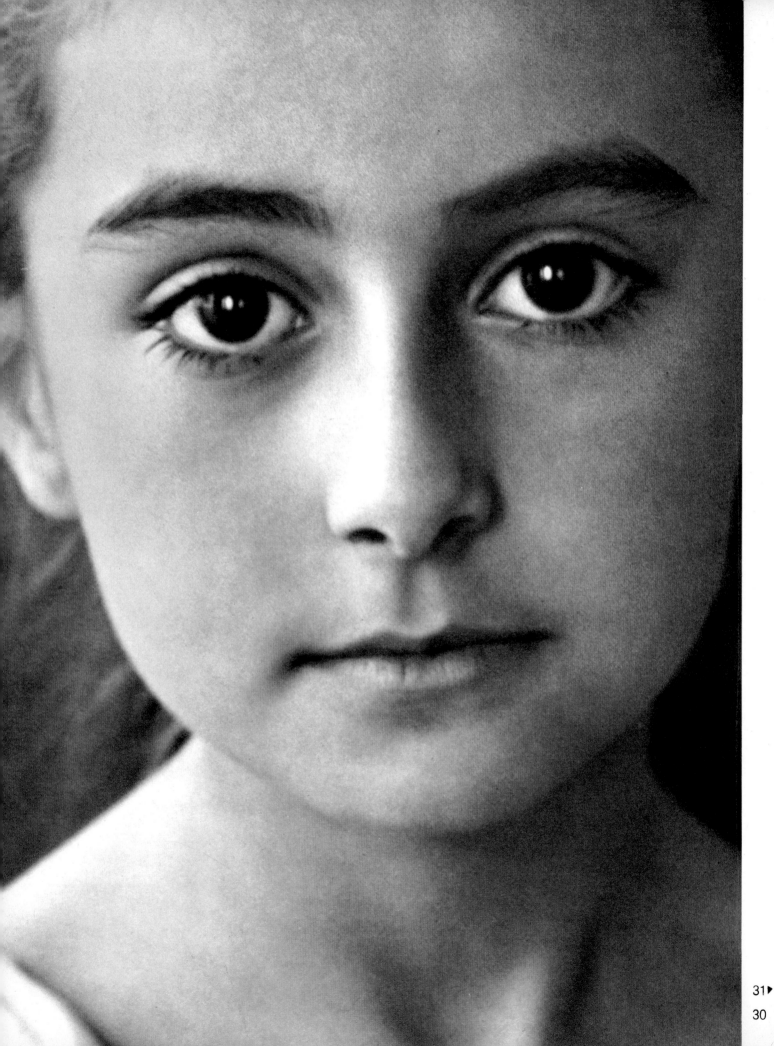

64

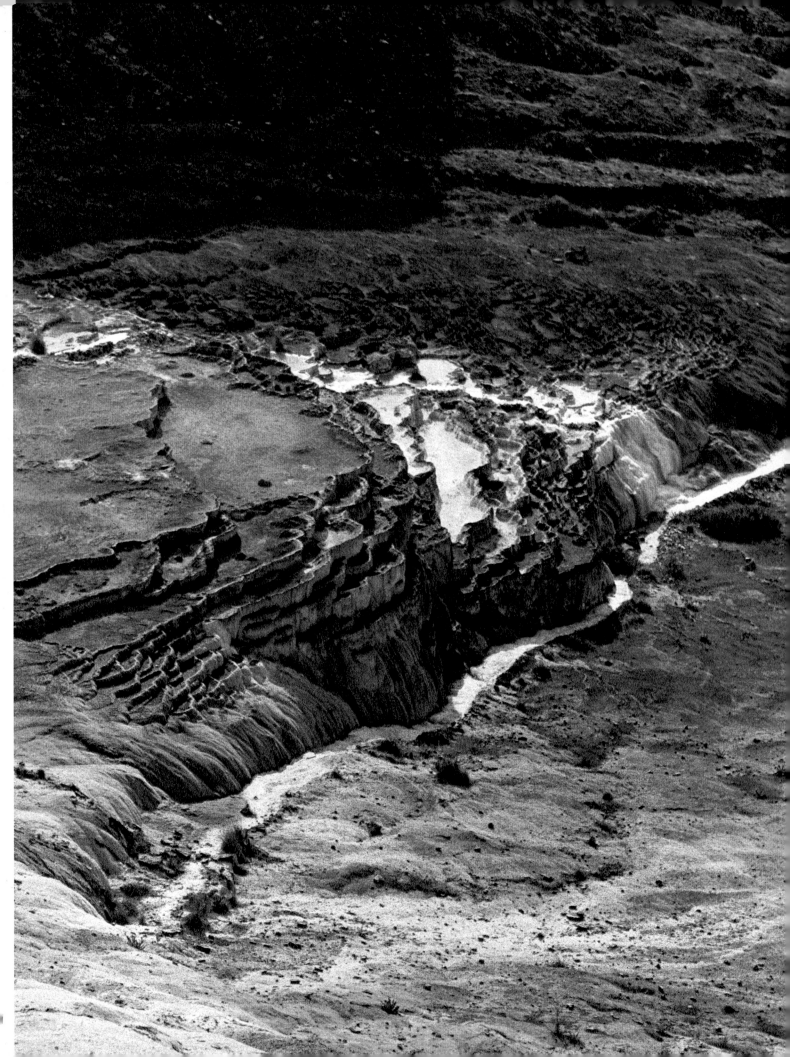

73

Photographers   Photo Numbers

S e a

GEORGIA

Samsun ○

○ Amasya

Ordu ○
○ Giresun

Trabzon ○
Rize ○

Artvin ○

Lake Cildir

Kars ○
Ani ○

○ Tokat

Yesil Irmak

○ Gümüsane

Coruh

A
R
M
E
N
I
A

Mount
Ararat
16,946 ft. △

○ Sivas

Erzincan ○

○ Erzurum

Agri ○

Dogubayazit ○

IRAN

D
O
C
I
A

L
I
A

Tunceli ○

Bingöl ○

Mus ○
Nemrut Daği
10,010 ft. △

Lake Van

Van ○

seri

Elazig ○

Lake Hazar

Bitlis ○

Aghthamar

as Dagi
~8 ft.

Malatya ○

K
A

Sürt ○

Hakkari ○

COMMAGENE

○ Adiyaman

Diyarbękir ○

Raman ○

Tigris

K U R D I S T A N

○ Maras

Euphrates

○ Mardin

yhan

Ceyhan

Urfa ○

A

○ Ceyhan

Gaziantep ☐

Haran ○

IRAQ

Iskenderun ○

*Lake
Amik*

Antakya ○

SYRIA

32 Tombstones with turbans on top designate the burial sites of dignitaries.

33 Street in the old section of Istanbul, a religious center in the last century. The ornamentation on the wall and tombstones dates from the Ottoman era.

34/35 Near this sphynx, a bas-relief sculptured out of Sançagözü gold, which is housed in the Hittite Museum at Ankara, there are bronze art treasures also belonging to the Hittite culture. Close to these are tombs from the Phrygian city, Gordium.

36 The main door of the Yeşil Cami (Green Mosque) at Bursa. (See photo 22 also.)

37 Contemporary painting of the Bazaar.

38 Old Ankara is clustered around the citadel to the north of the city which became part of the Ottoman Empire in 1414. The new city grew up in the plain on both sides of the railroad tracks which, in 1893, ran from Istanbul to Angora, as it was then called. There are still twenty towers standing on the citadel.

39 The mausoleum of Atatürk in Ankara. A marble monolith weighing forty-two tons covers the grave of the "Father of Modern Turkey."

40 Silk cocoons are gathered in their untied end threads. The woman lets them drip and passes them to the woman working next to her. This worker ties a knot in the threads and the cocoons are pulled down by the force of their own weight.

41 Antalya. Rug-weaver. Smyrna rugs, like Persian rugs, are double threaded. Every knot is wound around two warps. However, the carpets from Smyrna are stronger than the Persian carpets. The number of knots determines the price. (There may be 100,000 to 400,000 knots per square meter.)

42 The windmills of Bodrum, called Halicarnassus in ancient times, city of the Ionians on the Aegean Sea, residence of the king of Caria, and razed to the ground by Alexander the Great in 334 B.C. Birthplace of Herodotus. Nothing now remains of the famous mausoleum, one of the Seven Wonders of the World.

43 The columns of the Temple of Athena in Priene were destroyed by earthquakes. Beyond these overturned columns lies the plain of the great Maeander River (Büyük Menderes). Over the past millenium silt deposits, which continue to grow, have been formed by the shifting soil of the Bay of Latmos.

44/45 The amphitheater of Miletus, the most famous of the great monumental structures still preserved, used to hold 25,000 spectators. Constructed by the ancient Greeks, it was about three hundred feet long. It was subsequently completely restored by the emperor Trajan and surrounded with buildings.

46 Pergamum (Bergama). In the mid second century it was the capital of the mighty empire of Asia Minor. In 133 B.C. Attalus III, the last king, bequeathed it to the Romans, who made Roman-style additions to the Greek temples. The Temple of Serapis was transformed into a basilica in Christian times and dedicated to the Apostle John. The Seljuks captured the city and Tamerlane destroyed it. The relics of the Altar of Zeus can be seen in the Pergamum Museum in Berlin. They were excavated at the end of the nineteenth century with the help of a German archaeological team.

47 During the rainy months camel caravans can still be seen along the Aegean coast. In the highland areas the two-humped (Bactrian) camels are used instead of the one-humped dromedaries because they are heavier, more robust, and less sensitive to the cold.

48 Café in Bodrum (the ancient city of Halicarnassus) on the Aegean coast. The crusader castle of Saint Peter of the Hospitalers (Knight of Rhodes) can be seen in the background. In the fifteenth century the crusaders rebuilt the Seljuk fortress dating from the eleventh century, using the same stones.

49 Mevlâna's monastery in Konya, a dervish monastery dating from the thirteenth century and now converted into a museum. It contains collections from the Seljuk and Ottoman empires.

50 Peasant women often still wear the Turkish "baggy trousers." Since women were requested not to wear the veil, the head shawl has replaced it and gives protection against the heat, light, dust and ... curious glances!

51 The citadel of Anamur (Anemorium) on the Southern Anatolian coast was completed by the emirs of Karaman. The mosque was subsequently encircled by a building complex that is still standing today.

52 Cliff church at Göreme, near Kayseri.

53 The Göreme Valley. The fragile volcanic tufa, said to have come from Mount Erciyas, split and became fragmented from erosion. It was then covered with sedimentary rocks and eroded again. So the valley now looks like a lunar landscape. Around A.D. 600 a large number of cave settlements were established.

54 Göreme. The cliff dwellings carved into the soft rock are connected by inside passageways. This valley served as a retreat for the Christians. The Apostle Paul founded one of the first Christian churches here.

55 The Valley of the Pyramids – another characteristic sight in the Göreme district.

56/57 The city of Nevşehir in the middle of the "lunar landscape" formed of volcanic-tufa pyramids.

58 Entrance to a cliff church in the Göreme Valley. In the seventh century the Christians, threatened by the Arabs, had retreated from Kayseri into this tufa landscape. Most of the cliff churches date from the eleventh to thirteenth centuries. Some of the murals and frescoes are well preserved, especially where very little light has been able to penetrate.

59 A striking cliff chapel at Göreme.

60 Wrestling bouts at Edirne (Adrianople). During the Ottoman era the soldiers underwent vigorous physical training here before they were sent on expeditions to Europe. The Turkish wrestlers (called *pehlivan*) anoint their bodies with oil before the match.

61 Mount Erciyas (almost 13,000 feet), seen in late autumn from the district between Nevşehir and Aksaray. The name of the volcano has been changed several times. Today it is officially called Erciyas Daği in Turkey. (It is the Mount Argaeus of ancient times.)

62 Café in Yoran on the Aegean coast. The preparation of "Turkish" coffee, along with many Turkish recipes, is still maintained in the Balkans in spite of unpleasant memories of Turkish domination. Card-playing has replaced the old Turkish-Arabic chess games. The peaked cap is now worn instead of the outlawed fez.

63 A Turkish bath in Bursa dating from the Ottoman era. The Turkish custom of a hot steam bath followed by a massage also became popular in Europe.

64 Shoe vendor in the Istanbul Bazaar.

65 Street photographer in Izmir (Smyrna).

66/67 After every Muslim has completed his individual

▶Please fold out

prayers, the ceremony enters a collective phase and all worship together.

68 Ankara. Typical dress of the peasant women in Central Anatolia. In the background the minaret of the Arslanhane Mosque can be seen.

69 Performance at one of the typical traveling theaters.

70 Pamukkale (Hierapolis). Snow-white stalactite terraces formed by deposits of warm calcareous water over the centuries.

71 Pamukkale, where thermal water flows through.

72 Pamukkale. The warm springs contain carbonic acid and limestone. The water flows over the slopes and the carbonic acid evaporates. The limestone is deposited and forms these fantastic architectural patterns.

73 Pamukkale. (See text 70–72.)

74 Head of King Antiochus I on Nemrut Daği. The ruins of the Temple of Antiochus I, King of Commamagene (1st century B.C.), stand at a height of 8,205 feet in Southern Anatolia and can only be reached after a six-hour ride on muleback.

75 Temple of Zeus at Kütahya, southeast of Bursa. Famous ceramics are located in this place.

76/77 Aphrodisias (Geyre). The city flourished in the first and second centuries A.D. It was rewarded for its allegiance to Rome and exported its artistic works throughout the entire Roman Empire.

78 Tomb of the Macedonian king Amyntas, fourth century B.C., near Fethiye.

79 Annual fair at Germencik in Western Anatolia, where camel fights are held.

80 Near the modern city of Demre are the tombs of Limyra, dating from the fifth and fourth centuries B.C. The church and burial place of Saint Nicholas are also located in this district.

81 The hand-woven carrying bag is used in both Anatolia and the Balkans. Some old men often still prefer to wear a makeshift turban, but most men now wear a peaked cap since Atatürk banned the fez.

82/83 The Euphrates River near Eski Kahta, with its waters running low. After the snow melts, a huge tidal wave flows down from the Armenian mountains and annually threatens the dams in the Baghdad area. Even a water rat's hole can cause a dam to break. Thousands of people stand ready with sacks of sand to seal any apertures.

84 On Nemrut Daği stone statues erected to the deities stand about thirty feet high. They reflect a Greek-Oriental style.

85 In Eastern Anatolia wooded areas have become very sparse. Over a long period of time there were no restrictions on the felling of trees, and now erosion has washed the soil down into the valleys and distant plains of Mesopotamia. This naturally benefits the people in these districts who obtain their livelihood from the land, while the Anatolians suffer a loss. So the cliffs are now bare and present an iridescent landscape reflecting many pastel colors, similar to man's conception of the terrain on Mars.

86 Cavdarhisar near Kütahya, the old Roman city of Aesani. The Temple of Zeus.

87 Cavdarhisar. Amphitheater.

88 On the road from Ankara to Samsun – near Boğazköy. The relief carved into the cliff represents the marriage between the "Great God" and the "Great Goddess" and dates from the thirteenth – century B.C. Hittite civi-

lization. In Alcahöyük, about twenty miles east, are the tombs of the Hatti, predecessors of the Hittites.

89 Royal Gate at Hattuşaş near Boğazköy. The ramparts of the Hittite capital, Hattuşaş, are 3,300 years old. A tunnel fifty-five yards long leads under it.

90 The summit of Nemrut Daği is covered with small loose stones. This ancient historical site has been excavated by a group of American archaeologists. It is not easy to get to Nemrut, as it is a day's ride on muleback from the nearest village.

91 Ruins of the Temple of Antiochus I on Nemrut Daği.

92 Haran (formerly Charran) is situated in the Mesopotamian plain near the Syrian border. Haran is mentioned in Genesis 11:31–32 and 12:4–5 in connection with Abraham's travels from Ur to Canaan. The houses are built in such a way that they provide as much protection as possible against the extreme heat of this region. The holes in the walls allow the air to circulate.

93 In the vicinity of Konya shepherds have herded the sheep together so that the women may milk them. The cloths over the mouth replace the veil and serve as a dust filter.

94/95 Amasya, on the road between Ankara and the Black Sea, was the capital city of the king of Pontus. The royal palace and three burial vaults dating from the third and second centuries (Hellenic era) are still preserved. In the middle of this photo two thirteenth-century mosques can be seen.

96 The amphitheater at Side (near Antalya) was the largest in Pamphylia. It accommodated 13,000 people. Photo: part of a relief sculpture, copy of a theatrical mask worn by actors depicting the sileni and satyrs.

97 Termessos. There are many such burial grounds throughout Anatolia. Today, a nation whose prophet declared the worship of tombs to be heathen live surrounded by these cemeteries.

98 Lake Van in Eastern Anatolia lies at an altitude of nearly 6,000 feet and has no outlet. It is eight times as large as Lake Constance. The Armenian king Gagik Ardzrni had a church erected on the island of Aghthamar "around a cherry tree."

99 Wooden columns of the palace of Ishak Pasha near Doğubayazit, Armenia.

100/101 The Ishak Pasha palace in old Doğubayazit, dating from the late seventeenth and early eighteenth centuries. It is a strange mixture of Seljuk, Georgian, and Armenian architectural styles and a true symbol of the crossroads of many peoples.

102 Aghthamar. Angel sculptured in stone on the western side entrance of the Church of the Holy Cross, built from 915 to 921 by the Armenian king Gagik, who in 908 received the title of king from the Arabs and ruled over the kingdom of Vaspurakan on Lake Van. The reliefs in red sandstone depict scenes from the Old and New Testaments.

103 Mount Ararat (Ağri Daği), an extinct volcano, is the highest mountain in Anatolia and reaches a height of 16,946 feet. The snow level lies at about 14,500 feet. The alpine flora starts growing at about 8,000 feet. Glaciers extend deep down into the basins. According to Armenian legend, the remains of Noah's Ark still rest on the summit.

104 The Church of Saint Gregory of Honnentz at Ani, near Kars. Kars is perched at 6,000 feet above sea level.

Back Cover: Ancient wall inscription on the Eski Cami (Old Mosque) in Edirne.

Front Cover: The Blue Mosque in Istanbul.
Inside Front Cover: Hittite hieroglyphics (in the Ankara Museum).

1 Bursa. Construction of the Great Mosque (Ulu Cami) was begun in 1379 and completed in 1414. The prayer hall is topped by twenty domes, which are supported by twelve pillars. This is the oldest style of Turkish mosque and can be traced back to Arabic models.

2 The Great Covered Bazaar in Istanbul, situated in the old section of the city, where the Byzantine market used to be. This bazaar has repeatedly sustained fires followed by earthquakes. It covers an area of about 2,000,000 square feet.

3 Fishmonger on the Galata Bridge in Istanbul. This bridge separates the Golden Horn from the Bosporus.

4/5 View from the university tower of the Golden Horn and the Mosque of Suleiman the Magnificent (Süleymaniye Camii). Built by Suleiman I between 1550 and 1557. In the building complex there are many other domed buildings (including a Koranic school, library, baths, and kitchens where the poor can obtain food).

6 Mouth of the Golden Horn in the Bosporus. Mosque of Suleiman the Magnificent. To the left the Yeni Cami (New Mosque), which was built over a period of seventy years.

7 Cherry vendor in Antalya.

8 Over the past thousand years a type of woman designated as Levantine has emerged in the eastern Mediterranean region.

9 The Hilton Hotel in Istanbul with its honeycomb facade, which has proved so popular in sunny lands.

10 The Eyüp-Sultan Mosque was for a long time considered a holy site. It still calls to mind Aba Eyup Ensari, the sultan who died on this spot during the siege of Constantinople by the Arabs in the year 674. The mosque was built in 1458 by Mohammed the Conqueror. The tomb of Sultan Eyüp is covered with glazed tiles.

11 A crane flying round a minaret.

12 The Mosque of Sultan Ahmed. It is the only mosque with six minarets and has become known as the Blue Mosque because of its blue glazed tiles. It was built at the beginning of the seventeenth century, during the golden age of the Ottoman Empire, which then stretched from North Africa to Hungary.

13 A street in old Bursa. This city was founded in the second century B.C. by Hannibal when he was a guest of Prusias II. It fell into Roman hands when Lucullus defeated Mithridates of Pontus. After changing hands many times, Bursa eventually became the Ottoman capital. Today Bursa is known as a silk-manufacturing enter.

14 The Mosque of Sultan Ahmed at prayer time. The walls of the Blue Mosque are covered with blue and green tiles. Four massive pillars support the main dome.

15 A hadji (a Muslim who has made a pilgrimage to Mecca), scholar of the Koran, wearing a white turban and explaining the Koran to members of the faith.

16 The Blue Mosque in Istanbul. The domes are covered with lead tiles. In times of war these tiles were often replaced with sheets of copper because the lead was needed for other purposes.

17 Konya. The Mosque of Alâeddin Kaykubat (completed in 1221). Its mausoleum contains the tombs of eight Seljuk sultans. In the thirteenth century Konya was the Seljuk capital (capital of the Rum Empire).

18 Aya Sofia, masterpiece of Byzantine architecture. Completed in the seventh century and used as a Christian church until the capture of Constantinople by the Ottomans in 1453. They added minarets and the church was converted into a mosque.

19 The dome of the Blue Mosque in Istanbul (the Mosque of Sultan Ahmed). The Roman-arch windows, arranged one above the other in five rows, allow plenty of light to enter the mosque, making it one of the best illuminated.

20 Edirne (Adrianople). View from the southern minaret onto the domed roof of the hospital which forms part of the building complex in which the mosque is located.

21 The muezzin calls the faithful to prayer. "There is only one God and Mohammed is his prophet" ("Lla, illah-lla, Mohammed rasul Allah").

22 Bursa. Stonework on the wing of the door of the Yeşil Cami (Green Mosque). Completed in 1419 under Mohammed I. The stonemasonry above the main entrance depicts a section of the first sura of the Koran (Lead us on the right road...).

23 Konya. Dancing dervishes. Symbol of the path of the planets around the sun. Ecstasy and self-torture are part of their ritualistic practices. The dervishes were disbanded in 1925. Since then, they have held their ceremonies in private.

24 Istanbul. Behind the Aya Sofia is a district of old wooden houses. There is a rumor that there is no need to bother burning these houses down. It is simply a matter of waiting for the next fire. Turkish folklore states that nothing should be rebuilt in the place of a burnt house. But high building-costs are already a more effective deterrent to reconstruction than this superstition.

25 Konya. Old dwelling with the traditional divan, still a customary feature in Turkish homes. Sitting "tailor fashion" is the correct way to sit on it.

26 Sultan Suleiman the Magnificent (1520–1566) followed by two attendants. Under the reign of this sultan the Ottoman Empire attained its greatest period of glory.

27 This painting of Sultan Mohammed Fatih hangs in the Topkapi Castle (Topkapi Sarayi).

28 Flight of steps in Istanbul.

29 Istanbul. Belly dancer. The dance consists of rhythmic movements of the abdomen and hip muscles, while the rest of the body remains as motionless as possible.

30 A mixture of healthy lightheartedness and gentle melancholy, budding energy and fatalism characterizes the youth of today. In the Ottoman Empire fate (Kismet) could call every single Turk into the highest sphere of duty. In every Turk there was a potential pasha. But Turkish fatalism does not signify resignation. Europeans have interpreted this concept of destiny in a purely negative sense.

31 Topkapi Castle is considered one of the most important building complexes in the world. Construction of it began in 1465–1478 and was completed in the nineteenth century. Today it houses a museum (sultans' thrones, jewels, miniatures, fabrics, weapons, library, porcelain). Photo: sixteenth–century miniature with battle scenes from Europe.